Prepared to Be Positioned

Surrendering My Mess for a Message
Updated Edition

"For I know the thoughts that I think toward you, saith the LORD, thoughts of peace, and not of evil, to give you an expected end." Jeremiah 29:11

Katina L. Brown

Table of Contents

Thank You!

I'm so glad you have decided to read my book!

My degree is in Health Care Administration, not theology, so I don't pretend to be a Biblical expert. I can only say that God has placed the contents of this book on my heart through my personal relationship with Him.

I've had a book on my heart for many years, but I wasn't prepared to write it. Now that I am, God has positioned me to share it with you and I've poured my heart into expressing what God needs to come forth.

I've poured my heart into revealing my testimony so that someone will be closer to God because of it. I've relived experiences and emotions to be obedient to God, and I am blessed for doing it.

Be blessed in knowing that there is a message or messages in this book just for you. I have full confidence in God that those messages are intended for you to receive as a part of your preparation and/or positioning. I pray that you will embrace the messages with an open mind and use them for your growth in Christ.

May Christ richly bless you through my testimony and His Word!

Love in Christ, Katina

Introduction

What does "Prepared to be Positioned" mean?

Prepare
The action or process of getting something ready for use.
Spiritually speaking, getting ready to be used by God.

Position
To put or arrange (something) in a particular place or way.
Spiritually speaking, being put in a place to be used by
God.

Being prepared to be positioned means God gets us ready
to carry out His will and puts us in places to do it. This is
not a onetime occurrence, but a continual process
throughout life. Sounds simple, but many people don't get
this concept until later in their faith or quite frankly, never.
Why, because we are accustomed to believing that where
we are, what we have, and where we're going is because of
our own doing. By the way, this applies to church folks
too.

Yes, there are people in church who don't give God credit
during their everyday comings and goings; trials,
tribulations, joys, and triumphs. It's not because they are
bad people of faith, but because of where they are in their
faith. The people who don't give God the glory wonder
why they are in the same place year after year, not moving
into new positions in life or remaining in positions longer
than they think they should.

Ephesians 1:11-12 says, "In whom also we have obtained an inheritance, being predestinated according to the purpose of him who worketh all things after the counsel of his own will: That we should be to the praise of his glory, who first trusted in Christ."

Key Point: To the praise of His glory.

We can't be put in a place to be used by God without acknowledging that He is the one "keeping us" where we are and "taking us" into every season of life. I'm talking about daily confessions of faith and acknowledgement that **God is in the details**. We must acknowledge that He always has us in a particular place, for a particular reason, every single moment of every day.

Proverbs 16:1-4, 9 explains it well: "The preparations of the heart in man, and the answer of the tongue, is from the LORD. All the ways of a man are clean in his own eyes; but the LORD weigheth the spirits. Commit thy works unto the LORD, and thy thoughts shall be established. The LORD hath made all things for himself: yea, even the wicked for the day of evil."

Key Point: Commit thy works unto the Lord.

The reality is, there are our beliefs and ways of doing things, and THE TRUTH. God is TRUTH! When we surrender our way for THE TRUTH, we stop lying to ourselves. When we stop lying to ourselves, we become available for God to prepare and position, to take us from faith to faith in seasons He determines for His Glory. The Truth will always prevail!

"But we all, with open face beholding as in a glass the glory of the Lord, are changed into the same image from glory to glory, even as by the Spirit of the Lord." 2 Corinthians 3:18

Key Point: With open (able to be seen) faces.

Have you ever wondered why God doesn't just give all of us mansions with acres of land and large sums of money in the bank? Money would be one less thing we would have to worry about. Maybe you've wondered why God doesn't just prevent us from experiencing all the horrible things like losing a loved one, being abused, or being homeless. We know that He's able to do exceedingly above all that we ask Him to do!

The Bible says, our faith can move mountains! Why can't this wonderful loving God just move our mountains already! Take away the hardships! Maybe even give us a cure for cancer so that we can stop losing our loved ones to it! Why do we have to go through so many hardships when all we want to do is live, love God and love people?

If you are already living for Christ, maybe, just maybe you've thought of throwing in the towel because this daily Christian walk can be difficult sometimes. We could go back to living without being convicted in our spirits about doing the wrong things. We can distance ourselves from the people who try to keep us in line with the Word. If God would just move our mountains, we could simply tell people how great He is, RIGHT!

Oh, and by the way, did Job (from the Book of Job) really need to be tested until near death and couldn't God just give Sarah (from the book of Genesis) a baby up front? *Hmmmmm…..*

Biblical Perspectives

When we look to the Bible for guidance about why God doesn't always make everything nice and easy for us, the examples are plentiful! The Biblical examples show that God is strategic in His plans. He takes us from preparation to positioning for the uplifting of His Kingdom, which works for our good! Romans 8:28 says, *"And we know that all things work together for good to them that love God, to them who are the called according to His purpose."*

Sarah: Yes, God could have given Sarah a baby right away, His plan from the beginning was for her to give birth. However, Sarah's testimony teaches us that we can trust God to keep His promises and shows that He is an ALMIGHTY GOD! His plan was greater than meeting Sarah's needs, so her process had to be endured even though it was difficult and frustrating at times. By the time Sarah gave birth to Isaac, she was prepared to be positioned in the Bible as a woman teaching us what happens when we try to fix things on our own, a powerful testimony of perseverance and faith, and a constant reminder that there is NOTHING TOO HARD FOR GOD! *Genesis 16-18*

Job: The book of Job is an amazing detailed account of God giving satan power over all the possessions of a blessed man with good character, Job. He had a large family and many possessions. Satan used the power God allowed him to have by launching an outrageous attack on Job. In the end, Job was positioned as a Biblical example of how to remain humble when you have nothing but faith and the enemy is trying to take that too. Job didn't blame God and his character was not flawed even though all he saw was death and destruction, including the possibility of his own death.

Job worshipped and blessed God and finally God decided that Job was prepared to be positioned. The attack was over, and Job was positioned with twice as much as he had before. Today it is a compliment to be told that you have, "the patience of Job." Wow, what a way to be prepared and positioned by God!

The Book of Job

There are so many more Biblical examples (Ruth, Joseph, Paul, and David, to name a few that are most familiar.) of God preparing people for positioning. They represent us and our walk with Christ, in that their stories are like everyday experiences that we endure; relationship problems, difficulty having babies, getting in trouble with the law, fighting unimaginable battles and overcoming these obstacles with God if we surrender to Him.

God predetermined our paths. We are individually that important to Him. If we question the preparations, we are also questioning the positions He has waiting for us. We don't get to a place of positioning such as Job, by questioning God.

We must be able to surrender to God's will and get to a position where we can share with one another the profound greatness of God's love carrying us through life. After all, neither the preparation nor the position is solely for our own sake, but for us to testify and bring people closer to God.

Testify

"Come and hear, all ye that fear God, and I will declare what he hath done for my soul." Psalm 66:16

Our testimonies represent hope in God. This book includes my testimony, a personal account of being prepared to be positioned. I now know that God was always with me from the beginning of my life, even when I was hopeless. It is my responsibility to set aside fear of being vulnerable, and share my story for God's glory. *"I thought it good to shew the signs and wonders that the high God hath wrought toward me." Daniel 4:2*

I'm sharing my testimony because I believe that God has prepared and positioned me to do so for such a time as this. We all have a story, and my prayer is that you are blessed beyond measure from reading this book and that you will realize the power of your testimony! *"Howbeit Jesus suffered him not, but saith unto him, go home to thy friends, and tell them how great things the Lord hath done for thee, and hath had compassion on thee." Mark 5:19*

Psalm 107

'1 O give thanks unto the LORD, for he is good: for his mercy endureth forever. ² Let the redeemed of the LORD say so, whom he hath redeemed from the hand of the enemy; ³ And gathered them out of the lands, from the east, and from the west, from the north, and from the south. ⁴ They wandered in the wilderness in a solitary way; they found no city to dwell in. ⁵ Hungry and thirsty, their soul fainted in them.

⁶ Then they cried unto the LORD in their trouble, and he delivered them out of their distresses. ⁷ And he led them forth by the right way, that they might go to a city of habitation. ⁸ Oh that men would praise the LORD for his goodness, and for his wonderful works to the children of men! ⁹ For he satisfieth the longing soul, and filleth the hungry soul with goodness. ¹⁰ Such as sit in darkness and in the shadow of death, being bound in affliction and iron; ¹¹ Because they rebelled against the words of God, and contemned the counsel of the most High: ¹² Therefore he brought down their heart with labour; they fell down, and there was none to help.

¹³ Then they cried unto the LORD in their trouble, and he saved them out of their distresses. ¹⁴ He brought them out of darkness and the shadow of death, and brake their bands in sunder. ¹⁵ Oh that men would praise the LORD for his goodness, and for his wonderful works to the children of men! ¹⁶ For he hath broken the gates of brass, and cut the bars of iron in sunder.

^{17} Fools because of their transgression, and because of their iniquities, are afflicted. ^{18} Their soul abhorreth all manner of meat; and they draw near unto the gates of death. ^{19} Then they cry unto the LORD in their trouble, and he saveth them out of their distresses. ^{20} He sent his word, and healed them, and delivered them from their destructions.

^{21} Oh that men would praise the LORD for his goodness, and for his wonderful works to the children of men! ^{22} And let them sacrifice the sacrifices of thanksgiving, and declare his works with rejoicing. ^{23} They that go down to the sea in ships, that do business in great waters; 24 These see the works of the LORD, and his wonders in the deep. ^{25} For he commandeth, and raiseth the stormy wind, which lifteth up the waves thereof.

^{26} They mount up to the heaven, they go down again to the depths: their soul is melted because of trouble. ^{27} They reel to and fro, and stagger like a drunken man, and are at their wit's end. ^{28} Then they cry unto the LORD in their trouble, and he bringeth them out of their distresses. ^{29} He maketh the storm a calm, so that the waves thereof are still. ^{30} Then are they glad because they be quiet; so he bringeth them unto their desired haven.

^{31} Oh that men would praise the LORD for his goodness, and for his wonderful works to the children of men! ^{32} Let them exalt him also in the congregation of the people, and praise him in the assembly of the elders. ^{33} He turneth rivers into a wilderness, and the watersprings into dry ground; ^{34} A fruitful land into barrenness, for the wickedness of them that dwell therein.

³⁵ He turneth the wilderness into a standing water, and dry ground into watersprings. ³⁶ And there he maketh the hungry to dwell, that they may prepare a city for habitation; ³⁷ And sow the fields, and plant vineyards, which may yield fruits of increase. ³⁸ He blesseth them also, so that they are multiplied greatly; and suffereth not their cattle to decrease.

³⁹ Again, they are minished and brought low through oppression, affliction, and sorrow. ⁴⁰ He poureth contempt upon princes, and causeth them to wander in the wilderness, where there is no way. ⁴¹ Yet setteth he the poor on high from affliction, and maketh him families like a flock. ⁴² The righteous shall see it, and rejoice: and all iniquity shall stop her mouth. ⁴³ Whoso is wise, and will observe these things, even they shall understand the lovingkindness of the LORD.'

ENOUGH!

"And he arose, and rebuked the wind, and said unto the sea, Peace, be still. And the wind ceased, and there was a great calm."
Mark 4:39

I stood at my bedroom window, looking out, wondering why? Why am I here? I was only fourteen years old (even though until writing this book all my memories related to me being eleven years old), standing at my bedroom window contemplating to live or die. My drug addicted mother had come home in the middle of the night, woke me from sleep, and beat me. A man, a stranger that she brought home, pulled her off me saying, "ENOUGH!"

So I stood there, at the window, looking out into the darkness and at the concrete porch from the second floor of our apartment. I was unable to see what was next for me. I was unable to comprehend that there was already a plan in motion for my life before I was born. I could only see the darkness and the porch and the possibility of getting out of a place that was wounding my soul. I thought if I jumped out of the window I could either live or die. I could die and not have to live through mental and physical abuse anymore or I could live after the jump.

The thought of living in my neighborhood and living with my mother after trying to kill myself was more than I could take. I was more afraid to jump and live with the consequences! So, I decided to live! I now know that even as a 14-year-old girl, I gained clarity that night. I looked out of the window and said out loud, "Somebody please help me!" and I went to sleep. A few hours later, I woke up as usual, went to school as usual, but I found that it was going to be a very unusual day.

Born with Faith

"For I say, through the grace given unto me, to every man that is among you, not to think of himself more highly than he ought to think; but to think soberly, according as God hath dealt to every man the measure of faith." Romans 12:3

You see, what I didn't know at such a young age, is what Romans 12:3 tells me, I was born with a measure of faith given to me by God! I didn't know that Ephesians 2:10 says I was created on purpose for a purpose and that I was created by a God who knows my innermost thoughts (Psalm 139:2). I didn't know that I didn't belong to my mother, but Genesis 1:27 says I was created by God in His image and that 1 Timothy 4:4 says everything God created is good. But I know now!

The Bible clearly tells me that I was a child of God then and a woman of God now and I believe it! Today, as a woman of God, I can articulate my feelings from that night, but in that moment, all I knew were the simple thoughts of a child needing help. I had gone to church before, once a year on Easter Sunday, but I didn't know that I was born with faith. So that night at the window, I just stood there, tired, beaten, broken and asking somebody to help me. I never realized God was right there beside me. He kept me from jumping and got me up in the morning!

Joy Comes in the Morning

"For his anger endureth but a moment; in his favour is life: weeping may endure for a night, but joy cometh in the morning."
Psalm 30:5

Oh yes! The next day was very unusual! I was sitting in class, the principal walked in, my teacher pointed at me, and I went to the office where a man was waiting for me. I now know that he was from social services. He asked to see bruises on my body, showed me pictures of my bedroom, put me in his car, picked up my brother and sister in the same manner, left a note on my mother's front door telling her he had us, and drove us to a big building filled with people, papers, and desks!

I was confused, but calmly taking on the big sister roll. The man who was waiting for me in the office gave us juices and snacks, and waited for my mom to call. What they didn't know is that many times we would get home from school and had to walk to my grandmother's house because my mom wouldn't be home, so I had a feeling she wasn't going to call. They waited for her to call until they couldn't wait any longer. She never called.

One of the worst moments of my life happened next, my siblings and I were separated. I see it in my head like a movie scene, the screaming, and my siblings letting go of my hands as they were carried away. If I allow it, the hopelessness that I felt that day swells up in my throat, but God keeps me hopeful.

Faith Activated

"Now faith is the substance of things hoped for, the evidence of things not seen." Hebrews 11:1

We all have different ideas of what it means to be a strong person of faith. Adults usually equate someone's faith to how strong they appear in difficult situations. A child might think you are strong in faith when you go to church every Sunday. However, the faith that matters, is faith God sees.

What I've learned is, if God can't see your faith, it's not there. If God can't see your faith, you are operating in your own strength, and there are no benefits to that in your walk with God.

God sees our faith when we surrender and call out to Him, releasing our weakness for His strength, hoping that He is working things together for our good. His strength is made perfect in our weaknesses. He takes pleasure when we cry out to him in our distress. *2 Corinthians 12:8-10 says, "...My grace is sufficient for thee: for my strength is made perfect in weakness. Most gladly therefore will I rather glory in my infirmities, that the power of Christ may rest upon me. Therefore, I take pleasure in infirmities, in reproaches, in necessities, in persecutions, in distresses for Christ's sake: for when I am weak, then am I strong."*

This verse tells me that it's okay for me to surrender to God and let Him handle all my problems, concerns, and downright tsunamis. He is strong enough for all of us. I can rest at night knowing that I have put my faith in a God who, not only carries me, but all His children.

It was a long night after being separated from my siblings, but we were reunited the next day! God had showed up and showed out for the children He created on purpose with faith! I never lived with my mom again after being taken from school that day. My somebody helped me! My somebody was God!

Today I know that we are born with faith, and looking back on that traumatic time in my life, I realize that we must activate our faith. When I cried out for help, God heard me. God stepped in when I couldn't take it anymore. *1 Corinthians 10:13 says, "There hath no temptation taken you but such as is common to man: but God is faithful, who will not suffer you to be tempted above that ye are able; but will with the temptation also make a way to escape, that ye may be able to bear it."*

I activated my faith unknowingly and God moved on my behalf. He knew that day would come! He was waiting to take me into the next part of my journey. I got what I needed from those years in my life and it was time for me to move beyond them. So, I went to live with my cousin, who I would eventually call mom because she poured goodness into me and gave me a life worth living. The only problem is that when you go through a traumatic time as a child, you are not living as God created you to live (joyful, victorious, hopeful, and confident in Him). I had been "reprogrammed by the world" and my mother's circumstances. I believe my mother loved me, she just wasn't the sixteen-year-old that gave birth to me anymore; she too had been "reprogrammed by the world." The choices she made shifted her priorities and love, from her children to drugs. Therefore, my mindset was not of a child of God, but a child in survival mode dealing with adult problems.

Psalm 139:1-18

¹O lord, thou hast searched me, and known me. ²Thou knowest my downsitting and mine uprising, thou understandest my thought afar off. ³Thou compassest my path and my lying down, and art acquainted with all my ways. ⁴For there is not a word in my tongue, but, lo, O LORD, thou knowest it altogether. ⁵Thou hast beset me behind and before, and laid thine hand upon me. ⁶Such knowledge is too wonderful for me; it is high; I cannot attain unto it. ⁷Whither shall I go from thy spirit? or whither shall I flee from thy presence? ⁸If I ascend up into heaven, thou art there: if I make my bed in hell, behold, thou art there. ⁹If I take the wings of the morning, and dwell in the uttermost parts of the sea; ¹⁰Even there shall thy hand lead me, and thy right hand shall hold me. ¹¹If I say, Surely the darkness shall cover me; even the night shall be light about me. ¹²Yea, the darkness hideth not from thee; but the night shineth as the day: the darkness and the light are both alike to thee. ¹³For thou hast possessed my reins: thou hast covered me in my mother's womb. ¹⁴I will praise thee; for I am fearfully and wonderfully made: marvellous are thy works; and that my soul knoweth right well. ¹⁵My substance was not hid from thee, when I was made in secret, and curiously wrought in the lowest parts of the earth. ¹⁶Thine eyes did see my substance, yet being unperfect; and in thy book all my members were written, which in continuance were fashioned, when as yet there was none of them. ¹⁷How precious also are thy thoughts unto me, O God! how great is the sum of them! ¹⁸If I should count them, they are more in number than the sand: when I awake, I am still with thee.'

Transformed

"And be not conformed to this world: but be ye transformed by the renewing of your mind, that ye may prove what is that good, and acceptable, and perfect, will of God." Romans 12:2

Many women with similar testimonies can testify to this: The things that we see and experience can change us into people who go through life with wounded souls. Our God given identities become locked up in our past and our past take on identities of their own in our minds. That's why the Bible says be transformed by the renewing of your mind.

After going through ungodly experiences, we must be reprogrammed to a Godly mindset, the mindset God formed us with before we were in our mother's wombs (Jeremiah 1:5). When our minds are transformed by reading His Word, (The Word became flesh and dwelt among us John 1:14) we began to identify with who God created us to be as opposed to who the world changed us to be.

I know without question that I've been lost when I missed time reading God's Word, it's like walking around without my inner GPS. Being transformed by the renewing of our minds by reading God's Word is vital to the preparation and position God has for us.

Joshua 1:8 tells us to meditate on the Word, *"This book of the law shall not depart out of thy mouth; but thou shalt meditate therein day and night, that thou mayest observe to do according to all that is written therein: for then thou shalt make thy way prosperous, and then thou shalt have good success."* There is absolutely no substitute for how to renew your mind. God has given us an abundance of guidance in the Bible and we must follow it. *"So then faith comes by hearing and hearing by the Word of God." Romans 10:17*

I remember coming home from school one day and walking upstairs because I heard laughter coming from my mom's bedroom. I got to the door and my mom looked at me like she was disappointed that I was home. She immediately stopped playing with my sister, and I walked away with my head down. I never forgot that, it made me feel so deeply sad and socially unwanted.

That experience made it difficult for me to join in conversations. For many years, I felt like I would be rejected and I couldn't bare feeling the way my mom made me feel that day. In the process of being transformed by the renewing of my mind, I realized that the way she was treating me had everything to do with her and nothing to do with me. Her soul was troubled. When all is not well in a person's soul, they are not functioning in the capacity which God created them to function.

Now, Glory to God, His voice speaks to me louder than her voice. I feel loved and appreciated by my Father in Heaven, which supersedes all rejections, negative opinions, and anything else that I know does not represent God's love. Feeling transformed by God began in my heart and the more I learned His Word, transformation took place in my mind.

It was a process. Feeling loved by God can be an
immediate overwhelming relief, then, you slowly begin to
believe His promises as you grow more confident in Him
and your ability to love and be loved.

It's not easy erasing years of hurt and pain, but Philippians
4:13 says, *"I can do all things through Christ which strengtheneth
me."* There is nothing in this world that is too hard for God.
*John 16:33 says, "These things I have spoken unto you, that in me
ye might have peace. In the world ye shall have tribulation: but be
of good cheer; I have overcome the world,"*

Through the Valley

Psalm 23
"1The LORD is my shepherd; I shall not want.
*2 He maketh me to lie down in green pastures: he leadeth me beside
the still waters. 3 He restoreth my soul: he leadeth me in the paths
of righteousness for his name's sake. 4 Yea, though I walk through
the valley of the shadow of death, I will fear no evil: for thou art
with me; thy rod and thy staff they comfort me. 5 Thou preparest a
table before me in the presence of mine enemies:
thou anointest my head with oil; my cup runneth over. 6 Surely
goodness and mercy shall follow me all the days of my life:
and I will dwell in the house of the LORD forever."*
Amen!

Living with my cousin, a nurse, was a totally different
world. We had food in the refrigerator every day. I had
better quality clothes, and just an overall better life, but I
was still feeling the effects of my troubled childhood.

I began having the most horrible dreams of a man stabbing me in the stomach. I would scream so loud that the neighbors would ask my cousin if I was okay the next day. She would walk me from room to room in the middle of the night just to reassure me that no one was there.

I didn't know it then, but I was walking through a dark valley. God was there, but I couldn't see Him. I couldn't feel His love yet. So, I began looking in other places for that love.

I was trying to feel the love God created me to feel, but through other people. However, like many girls and women who don't know God's love, I would only find conditional love. Today I know that there is no love greater than God's unconditional love! *"For God so loved the world, that he gave his only begotten Son, that whosoever believeth in him should not perish, but have everlasting life." John 3:16* That is a love so forgiving and pure that it will never be found in any human being!

Looking for Love

"And hope maketh not ashamed; because the love of God is shed abroad in our hearts by the Holy Ghost which is given unto us."
Romans 5:5

It was almost as if someone said, on your mark, get set, go! When my cousin worked or after school, I'd go to my grandmother's house sometimes. One day, I met my "first love." One of my male cousin's best friends. I was laying on my grandmother's sofa when he walked over to me, looked at me with interest, and began paying attention to me every day after that. That's all it took!

I was 14 years old and I think he was 16. It didn't take long before I was sneaking around to be with him and eventually became pregnant with my first child. I had an abortion, which I don't say light heartedly. As a young girl, you don't realize the impact this will have on your life. He never knew that I was pregnant.

I continued being a rebellious teenager, sneaking around with him every chance I got. I loved him; I thought I needed him because he said he loved me. I was pregnant by him again at 16, but this time was different. He told his mom about the baby, and they were excited. I was excited too. I was going to have a baby, but that pregnancy sadly ended in an abortion too.

I went to one of his family gatherings after the abortion. His mom looked at me and said, "Why did you abort my grandchild?" I was so devastated and broken because I realized in that moment, a baby was being missed and it was my baby and my fault. I was ashamed and embarrassed. I immediately left the party and a part of me felt gone.

I lost my joy. I didn't feel like a good person after that. The worst part is I felt like I couldn't talk about it, and that I had done something so horrible, I deserved whatever I was feeling.

If I could talk to the sixteen-year-old me today I would say, "I'm so sorry you had to endure those agonizing procedures and the pain you felt for causing other people's pain." I would say, "This is only a season, God is watching over you, you are not alone, you are loved, and this too shall pass." I would also tell myself to be more responsible, but, we can't go back and talk to our troubled selves.

God is with Us

"Let your conversation be without covetousness; and be content with such things as ye have: for he hath said, I will never leave thee, nor forsake thee."
Hebrews 13:5

God is very clear when He said He will never leave us. One of the most interesting aspects of the Word of God is that you have the choice to believe it or not. I choose to believe that He will always be with me. The other option is not believing and lacking faith, lacking true love, and lacking a savior who was sent for me to have an abundant life. Glory to God for giving us a way to Him. A way to live a life filled with His love. He sent His only son, Jesus Christ, to die on the cross for us to live a life filled with hope and a promise for brighter days.

I want to tell you right now, God is always with you. He is with you when you feel hopeless. If you are going through a divorce, God is with you. He is with you during financial setbacks and the inability to pay bills. He is with you when you are sick, healing you according to His will for your life. He is with you! He is with you when you have lost everyone. He's always with us, even when we make the biggest mistakes of our lives.

When you feel alone, read the Bible, you'll always find an "on-time" Word from the Lord! I didn't know that God was with me during my teenage years, so I grew more and more depressed after aborting my babies. No one noticed that I was taking my lunch to the bleachers in high school, eating alone and becoming increasingly sad. I didn't want to go to school. In fact, I wanted to die. I felt so alone even though I knew my cousin loved me.

I knew there was a gun in the house, so one day I decided that I was done living and there I was again, in another life or death situation. I went into my bedroom and prepared the gun to shoot myself in the head! Just as I raised the gun to my head, my cousin walked in. GOD SHOWED UP AGAIN!

You see, I didn't lock the door because she rarely came into my room and I thought she would come in after she heard the shot, BUT GOD sent her in. She took the gun out of my hand, took it outside, and fired the bullet into the sky.

I was still alive again, if only I'd known then that God had a plan for my life. I was too broken to see it. When you have two abortions, especially at such a young age, the negative voices in your head are loud. What would your child look like? You are an awful person! How could you kill those babies! The voices began to monopolize mind.

I felt like I couldn't talk about my feelings, especially not the babies because they were gone, not real, but they were real to me. I experienced the confusing (at such a young age) symptoms from a life growing inside of me. I was at a very low point, but by the grace of God I kept going.

"And he said unto me, My grace is sufficient for thee: for my strength is made perfect in weakness. Most gladly therefore will I rather glory in my infirmities, that the power of Christ may rest upon me." 2 Corinthians 12:9

Building Trust

"Lead me in thy truth, and teach me: for thou art the God of my salvation; on thee do I wait all the day." Psalm25:5
"Cast thy burden upon the LORD, and he shall sustain thee: he shall never suffer the righteous to be moved." Psalm 55:22

Trusting God is everything to me now because I know what it's like to keep my emotions bottled up. All my fears, hurts, and insecurities were being kept inside. I've been in that dark place where I felt like I couldn't trust anyone. I would write poems about being trapped in a mind that embraced my every thought. I felt like a captive in my own mind, and it took the love of God to set me free.

Being trapped is not an option when you surrender to God. He tells us to cast all our cares upon Him because He cares for us. This is the epitome of faith, trusting Him to take care of you. Trusting Him to know what you need. Trusting Him to bring it to pass. It's not easy when you have consciously built a wall to protect yourself, but God is already on the side of the wall that you are on. He already knows what you need. He's just waiting for you to reach out to Him. He has made provisions for every step of our journey.

When we trust God, we see our fears lessen, pains weaken, and our insecurities manifest into strengths. At the same time, we know that it's ok to have weaknesses because God's strength is made perfect in our weakness.

I would reflect on my past and wonder how I made it out of certain situations, now I know without a doubt that God was with me. So, when I look back over my life, I see a God who cares for me, which makes it easier for me to understand how I kept going. I graduated high school, worked, attended college and by the age of twenty-one enrolled in nursing school.

Things were looking up for me. I wasn't with my "first love" anymore. I had a new love, of course. In fact, I had a couple of new loves by then. I thought I was moving past the deep seeded pain in my soul, but as many of us know, our issues will always resurface with much greater force until we deal with them.

I was doing well in nursing school when God placed an Air Force Reservist, one of my nursing teachers, in my life. She told me about the benefits of joining the Air Force and I was intrigued. I was always one of the top students, until I was once again pregnant! I know, I should have used protection EVERY TIME, but I didn't. I'm convinced that I didn't love myself enough to protect myself!

This pregnancy was different though, I was going to have my baby. I was looking forward to redeeming myself! It's so hard to share with everyone that I terminated that pregnancy too. It breaks my heart to share that, but I'm in God's strength sharing this with you.

As I lay on the table and the doctor suctioned out the baby, through the fog of the medication that was supposed to relax me, I said "My Baby!" My heart was broken! I was mourning the loss of the baby I had decided to carry, but didn't. Why did I do it? I didn't follow my heart! I couldn't even bathe myself because I was in such a deep depression.

Struck Down but Not Destroyed

"We are troubled on every side, yet not distressed; we are perplexed, but not in despair; Persecuted, but not forsaken; cast down, but not destroyed; Always bearing about in the body the dying of the Lord Jesus, that the life also of Jesus might be made manifest in our body. For we which live are always delivered unto death for Jesus' sake, that the life also of Jesus might be made manifest in our mortal flesh. So then death worketh in us, but life in you." 2 Corinthians 4:8-12

If we look at everything from a Godly perspective, would we have fewer problems? No, we wouldn't have fewer problems, but we would know that the problems will not overtake us. We would definitely make better decisions.

Sometimes it's hard to look at things from a Godly perspective because we would have to do as Proverbs 3:6 says, *"In all thy ways acknowledge him, and he shall direct thy paths.*" We would have to trust God to direct our paths, which is a great thing to do, but it requires complete trust and continued preparation for where He is taking us. It requires growth in our faith in God.

We say we trust God but many of us are often reluctant to put total trust in God. I'm not judging because I have been guilty of saying I trust God, but not completely trusting Him. In fact, I was a repeat offender at one time. However, I've learned that everything is not always what it seems and a Godly perspective tells me like it is. This level of faith doesn't happen overnight.

I missed a nursing exam when I had the last abortion, and when I went to retake the exam, I failed it. I failed out of nursing school because I had been irresponsible. I was embarrassed, devastated, and depressed! I always said I left school for the military because I didn't want to face the reality. The reality is, I was still bleeding, emotionally unstable, and devastated about having another abortion. I clearly hadn't studied well, so I failed the test. I felt like a failure all over again. Maybe you can relate. I was so lost!

I walked out of the school, got into my car and drove. I just drove, still in my student nursing uniform. I drove from Tampa to Orlando until I finally stopped. I don't think I thought of anything during the entire ride, if I did, it must have been a million thoughts and they all ran together.

I used my rent money to check into a hotel. I didn't have a plan. I didn't know what to do! God had to be with me because I was, in every sense of the phrase, A HOT MESS!

I fell asleep, got up the next morning without a plan, and began driving again. I ended up at a beautiful park. I sat there looking at the water and the animals. It was in that moment that I felt a sense of peace. I didn't recognize it as peace, but that's exactly what it was, God's peace that surpasses all understanding. I wasn't what I would have normally been, in the bed crying, trying to make sense of it all. I was resting in His glorious peace. He'd done it again, saved me from myself and I didn't even recognize His presence! I knew of God, but I didn't have a relationship with Him.

Pressing Forward

"I press toward the mark for the prize of the high calling of God in Christ Jesus." Philippians 3:14

I don't think I thought of my next steps or what I was going to do in that moment at the park. I just watched the ducks in the water, the birds flying, kids playing, couples laughing, and life continuing. I stayed at the park under a tree looking around most of the day. Afterwards, I decided to drive home and I joined the Air Force shortly after that day.

The day after my 22nd birthday, in 1994, I boarded a plane to boot camp. I left Tampa, but took my troubled soul with me! I was a little older than most new Airmen, so I had higher rank and a little more pay. I was happy. I felt free, the most grown up I had ever felt. I was ready to

31

make this work and forget the past. I would soon meet a man; I was still looking for that love or someone to validate me.

Years passed and at 25 years old I was pregnant with his child. Our baby boy was born beautifully and healthy in 1997. It was an amazing experience, which brought me tremendous joy! I would learn right away that I was prepared for that position. I knew my baby needed me and I was determined to love him and be strong for us.

It was hard being a single parent, financially and emotionally. I would tell girls and young women to wait until you are married, but that's not how my story goes. I was prepared to be a mom and I loved my son more than anything in the world.

I had attended church several times before getting pregnant and by the grace of God even though I'd go after a night of partying, I sat in the back and absorbed the messages God was giving me. Those messages made me stronger and stronger. Those messages made me aware that I was never alone. They were messages of hope and strength to trust myself to love my baby. I was being transformed by the renewing of my mind, slowly but surely. Even though I Hadn't recognized Jesus as My Lord and Savior yet, God was preparing me for the position of knowing Jesus. I wasn't chasing love, but love was there for me!

A New Path

"For I know the thoughts that I think toward you, saith the LORD, thoughts of peace, and not of evil, to give you an expected end." Jeremiah 29:11

I was doing well, taking care of my son, working, and feeling better than I'd felt in a long time. I was done drinking and partying and that was great! I was alone and fine with it. For the first time in a long time, I wasn't looking for love. That is, until my girlfriend introduced me to a military man, single parent of a 3-year-old beautiful daughter.

We met in February of 1998, married in August 1998, and moved to Italy in 1999. Suddenly, God had blessed me with a husband and two children in a country people dreamed of visiting. My blessings were too many to count, and only God could have given them to me. *"Now unto him that is able to do exceeding abundantly above all that we ask or think, according to the power that worketh in us," Ephesians 3:20*

We lived in a beautiful Italian home and fell in love with all the beauty Italy had to offer. Castles, food, and shopping! We immediately began going to church and the military church community embraced us right away. I would soon accept Christ into my life. The best decision I've ever made. My life changed even more drastically! I had a family and Jesus!

Having Christ in my life was the missing piece. I had the unconditional love I'd been searching for. I felt connected to my Heavenly Father! For the first time in my life, I felt purposeful and filled with hope. It felt natural to say, "I Love the Lord" because I learned that He loved me first! I realized that He always loved me.

I finally understood what I'd learned once a year in church as a little girl, "Jesus loves me this I know, for the Bible tells me so." I never needed to search for love because it was always there to guide me along the right path. But as they say, "When you know better you do better" or "When you know better you should do better." So, I did.

Knowing how much God loves me and forgives me gave me a great sense of peace and resolve about everything that I had gone through. I shared my testimony about standing at the window, to an entire congregation of people. I started to become a whole person. When I looked in the mirror I could see the inside of me connecting with the outside. I began to feel good about who I was as a person. I forgave myself for having the abortions. I forgave myself for making bad decisions in life. I forgave myself because God forgave me.

The Lord began to heal me; after all, He is the Lord that heals (Exodus 15:26). The healing began when I understood that God had not given up on me and He was with me every step of the way. I began to feel like I was of value, especially to God. I was positioned to be of use for God and I was excited to be of service. His love was evident and it not only kept me going, but also gave me a new-found energy for life! I was being prepared for my next position, to deal with my issues for His glory!

Dealing with My Issues

I cried a lot after initially giving my life to Christ. There was so much hurt and pain that I had never addressed. I was being prepared for my next position; the next level of my faith.

Dealing with my issues was a part of the process. I began peeling away deep layers of pain associated with my issues. My issues had taken root in my soul, and other issues stemmed from that root.

I had to begin the process of uprooting those dead negative memories and impressions of myself; self-doubt, low self-worth and the heavy burden of guilt associated with aborting my babies. I began to understand the root of my depression. I had a lot of questions and, as you know, God had answers!

As I worked to dig up that painful root, I found myself asking God, WHY? I had questions that only He could answer. I needed concrete answers to build a solid foundation of faith.

There is no substitute for communicating and crying out to God for answers. I was direct with God about what I needed from Him, and He heard my cries.

I asked God:

Why did you give me to a mom who didn't love me enough to say no to or quit using drugs?

Why did you, God, let me go through such horrible times?

Where were you when I needed you?

How can I truly heal?

What do I do now, among all these people who seem to have themselves so well put together? Can't they see right through me and see everything I went through!

At that time, I didn't know how to be still and listen to God speak to me, and that was okay at the time. God would answer my questions through gospel songs, church sermons, women's fellowship, and other Christian's testimonies. However, most of my answers came from reading the Word of God! There wasn't one question I couldn't find the answer to in the Bible! Not One!

His answers were clear! He told me that He loved me so much that He gave His only son for me to live free of shame and guilt (John 3:16)! He told me that even though I wept a lot, He made sure to give me some joyous times (Psalm 30:5)! He always brought some form of joy so that I could breathe. He knew that one day I would use that breath to praise Him (Psalm 150:6).

He told me that when I was hungry, He provided food for me to eat (Psalm 107:9). He told me that when men beat my mother, He protected her to protect me, and that I was always safe (Psalm 18:2). He told me not to let my heart be troubled (John 14:1) and to continue along the path of righteousness because in due season I would reap what I've sown if I don't give up (Galatians 6:9).

I was so encouraged by what God was telling me that I began reading the Bible without crying. His joy was taking over and becoming my strength. I learned so much more about how much He loved me. John 3:1 says, *"Behold, what manner of love the Father hath bestowed upon us, that we should be called the sons of God: therefore the world knoweth us not, because it knew him not."*

I learned that the world will never love me the way I need to be loved, because greater is He that is in me than He that is in the world (1John 4:4). Before I knew it, my foundation was formed, and that's something that will never change. It's in me now and no matter what happens in my life God's love will always reveal itself because love conquers all!

More than a Conqueror

Romans 8:31-39

[31] What shall we then say to these things? If God be for us, who can be against us? [32] He that spared not his own Son, but delivered him up for us all, how shall he not with him also freely give us all things? [33] Who shall lay any thing to the charge of God's elect? It is God that justifieth. [34] Who is he that condemneth? It is Christ that died, yea rather, that is risen again, who is even at the right hand of God, who also maketh intercession for us. [35] Who shall separate us from the love of Christ? Shall tribulation, or distress, or persecution, or famine, or nakedness, or peril, or sword? [36] As it is written, for thy sake we are killed all the day long; we are accounted as sheep for the slaughter. [37] Nay, in all these things we are more than conquerors through him that loved us.

[38] For I am persuaded, that neither death, nor life, nor angels, nor principalities, nor powers, nor things present, nor things to come, [39] Nor height, nor depth, nor any other creature, shall be able to separate us from the love of God, which is in Christ Jesus our Lord.

At this point in my life I knew that I had it going on, I was more than a conqueror! Yeah right, far from having it going on. I was still dealing with issues, trying to figure myself out while raising kids and being married. You don't become some super human woman of God where nothing can get you off track or upset, ever.

What you become, if you make your relationship with God a priority, is a Woman of God, more and more like Christ. You begin to display what's taking root in your soul, and God had taken root in my soul. In fact, I began to look forward to opportunities to show the God in me and display The Fruits of the Spirit. *"But the fruit of the Spirit is love, joy, peace, longsuffering, gentleness, goodness, faith, meekness, temperance: against such there is no law." Galatians 5:22-23*

When you make your relationship with God a priority, you begin to grow in Christ. Each level of growth has its own preparation and positions, trials and tribulations, messages from God, and new opportunities to develop your faith and mature for God's glory.

Preparation is a process! We can say, "If I knew then what I know now," but we weren't meant to know then what we know now. The preparation you went through for now is different from what you went through for then. Embrace the position God has you in today and glorify Him, so that

He can use you effectively while preparing you for your next position.

Preparation and positioning is so powerful because it's constant throughout life. God doesn't say there are a certain number of faith levels. 2 Corinthians 3:18 says, *"But we all, with open face beholding as in a glass the glory of the Lord, are changed into the same image from glory to glory, even as by the Spirit of the Lord." He says we go from faith to faith!*

We go from faith to faith. God is ordering every step of faith and He decides when to take us to the next level. Your faith should become stronger and more useful. You should be able to look back over your life and say, look at what the Lord has done for me! I am more than a conqueror through Christ Jesus! He's the Power and the Glory forever and ever, AMEN! He's my Heavenly Father!

The Lord's Prayer

Matthew 6:9-13

[9] *"This, then, is how you should pray:*
"'Our Father in heaven,
hallowed be your name,
[10] *your kingdom come,*
your will be done,
on earth as it is in heaven.
[11] *Give us today our daily bread.*
[12] *And forgive us our debts,*
as we also have forgiven our debtors.
[13] *And lead us not into temptation,*
but deliver us from the evil one.

Forever! Amen!

Peeling Away the Layers

"The glory of this latter house shall be greater than of the former, saith the LORD of hosts: and in this place will I give peace, saith the LORD of hosts." Haggai 2:9

I was intent upon learning as much as possible about being a woman of faith. I continued being delivered from the bondage of my past. As I peeled away layer after layer, God decided that it was time for the harder work to be done! He was ready for me to peel away the deepest layer of my past. It was time for me to truly understand that greater is He that is in me than He that is in world (1 John 4:4).

I was prepared! My foundation was rooted in Christ. I was ready for whatever I was about to face, besides what could be worse than what I had already gone through! I believed God for His Word. I trusted Him for a better life and continued moving forward. *"The glory of this latter house shall be greater than of the former, saith the LORD of hosts: and in this place will I give peace, saith the LORD of hosts." Haggai 2:9*

I was also vulnerable! It hadn't registered yet, that I would be persecuted for righteousness' sake (Matthew 5:10). They don't sing that in songs and if I read it, I skipped right over that part! So, one of the most painful areas of my life was waiting to be healed, and because God is so good I never knew it was there. A storm was brewing for my good! This is what happened:

I was still in Italy and all of a sudden over about a two-week period there were multiple fatal car accidents

41

involving the local community and military families. This included a young man who had just joined the Air Force and was in our welcome to Italy class when we arrived. We had lunch with him in a group setting. He sat next to my husband and across the table from me to the left.

I can still picture his face, a tall dark-skinned kid (He was a kid to me), with a skinny frame. He was quiet, but I could tell that he was excited to be new to the military and Italy. When I learned that he died during one of the car accidents, it weighed heavy on my heart.

I think there were seven car accidents before I began to feel depressed. I learned that the car accidents and the emotions they evoked in me, triggered what was deep inside of me needing to be healed. I'm still amazed by that!

My emotions grew stronger after every accident. Until one day, the man who was in my dreams years ago, became someone I was face to face with. I went home from work one day and became paralyzed with fear. I crawled under the comforter in my bed and was scared to come out from under it. I felt like I was losing my mind. I kept thinking that this man, who wasn't really there, was going to "get me."

My husband helped me through that night and the next day I reported for duty. I was a medic, so I was in the medical building, which housed several clinics. I became more and more mentally unstable with each passing second. I went into one of the mental health worker's office and told him I needed help. He calmly walked me over to the mental health clinic and within the hour I was with a psychologist.

The doctor and I talked a lot, and what I realized changed my life! All the memories and pain flooded back into my mind and it took weeks of therapy to deal with it. During a series of questions, the doctor reached my core. The root of my pain was being raped when I was five years old.

The man in my dreams, the man I feared, was real. He had taken me to the beach when I was five years old. He and his girlfriend brought me back to an apartment where I remember the lamp falling, him chasing me around the room, eventually catching me and raping me.

I'm sharing this very personal story because we must understand that who we are, how we treat people, and how we allow ourselves to be treated, stems from what has taken root in our souls. If you have become anything other than who God says you are (in the Bible), it's important to acknowledge it and deal with it.

We cannot mask pain and fear forever. We must heal our souls. Otherwise, we develop characteristics or allow others to impose upon us the many different characteristics stemming from deeply rooted unresolved issues; bullying, mean girl mentality, selfishness, depression, restlessness, unhealthy habits or self-sabotaging habits, materialistic, resentful, angry, and/or sad.

Thankfully, God prepared me to deal with the hurt of my past. He had graciously suppressed it until I was strong in Him and prepared to deal with it. I prayed and prayed, and sought refuge in God. It would have been easy to hide under my comforter and be the victim, but as a Woman of God, I knew I had to walk by faith and allow God to heal me in His timing.

I worked through the pain of being raped and molested. I've worked through the pain of feeling less than other women because of what was in my soul. I've worked through the pain of so many things that kept me from being the woman God created me to be. I continue to work through my issues with God because He tells us to continue to work out our salvation with fear and trembling of Him (Philippians 2:12).

It's not easy knowing that I was abused, but I accept that it was a part of my journey. So, it really is easy to praise God anyway! I make conscious decisions to allow His love to define me, not my past. I strive to be stronger in Christ one day at a time.

I pressed forward in my new life with Christ and became pregnant again. I graduated with my bachelor's degree while I was pregnant, and eventually gave birth to my second child, a healthy baby boy. Then, surprise, 15 months later came a healthy baby girl. I would end up giving birth to three children, one in Nebraska, Italy, and another in New Jersey, which is where we moved after four years in Italy.

I know that God gave me a second chance, so I've poured Godly love into all my children. They represent the unconditional love of God in my life! They represent the profound Word of God, because I love Him, He is working ALL things together for my good (Romans 8:28)!

God has placed me in a position to write and share my testimony so that I can have the greatest impact in spreading His profound message of being prepared to be positioned. To share that everything we go through is known to Him. He will bring us to each position for which we were created, if we stay on His path.

God's Word is true, what the enemy meant for bad, God will turn it around for our good (Romans 8:28). Thank God I'm in a position to testify. I thank God that I am in a position to help others heal. I thank God that I am in a position to glorify Him! I thank God I was prepared for the position of standing on The Rock of My Salvation for His light to shine through me and draw others to Him!

Our Souls Are Real

"My soul, wait thou only upon God; for my expectation is from Him." Psalm 62:5

Many years later, on October 26, 2016, I was standing in my kitchen cutting potatoes to cook in green beans for church, so a lot of potatoes. I began daydreaming about being on Super Soul Sunday with Oprah. She would come to my home and meet my family.

I was wondering what I would offer her, lemonade or ice water. I was seriously daydreaming. Then, and this is why I rushed to write this down and decided to include it in my book, Oprah asked me, "What do you know for sure?" All of a sudden, my dreaming became real.

I felt like, whoa, that's a real-time question. I was forced to answer in my conscious state of mind. So, I continued cutting potatoes and thinking about sitting there with her and almost in tears, I answered.

I said, "What I know for sure is that our souls are real, my soul is real." I said, "Our souls are real and when they are wounded, they need time and ATTENTION to heal. When they are joyful, THAT JOY MUST BE NURTURED. When our souls are loving, LET THEM LOVE AND BE LOVED." Then, I was finished cutting the potatoes, but I wasn't finished experiencing that spiritually charged moment of answering her question.

I thought, "Our souls are real and if we could wake up and start the day recognizing the condition of our soul, maybe we would be more likely to give it what it needs." I said to myself out loud, "Oh that's good I have to write that in my book and maybe Oprah will read it one day."

What must have been the condition of my soul as I went through my childhood? My soul was wounded from being raped, and every negative experience after that made the wound more difficult to heal. Many years later, I still wasn't aware that my soul was wounded, but it showed in my decisions.

Everybody has a story. Some so horrible you wouldn't want to hear or read. Many souls are wounded, and we can't be put in a position to help others if we don't take care of ourselves.

Lately I've been trying to stay away from anything that disturbs my peace. I've been spending more time reading God's Word. Last year, I went on a one week get away by myself, at the beginning of the school year, which is unheard of for me. I stayed in a hotel on the beach and I was just Katina. Best birthday present ever!

So, taking into consideration how I've been treating myself and others, I would say that all is well within my soul. I'm prepared for the position I'm in today. God prepared and positioned me to testify in my book; to reach more people for His glory.

I was diagnosed with Lupus in 2015. I'm sick, but my soul doesn't feel sick. I'm exhausted, but my soul feels energetic. My soul is healed! It's empowering to know that the little girl in me is healed. She's at peace. She won! She survived! That's a breakthrough and a weight lifted. Isn't it amazing what recognizing the condition of your soul can do? It's almost like getting a medical diagnosis, acknowledging the problem, and fixing it.

Beauty for Ashes

"To appoint unto them that mourn in Zion, to give unto them beauty for ashes, the oil of joy for mourning, the garment of praise for the spirit of heaviness; that they might be called trees of righteousness, the planting of the LORD, that he might be glorified." Isaiah 61:3

The hardest part of letting go of a hurtful past is accepting it for what it was. If it was painful, acknowledging the pain is equally painful. If it was confusing, acknowledging the confusion can be just as confusing. If it was disgusting, the disgust becomes defined, and it is hard to accept that you lived through disgust.

I remember my mom calling me a "hussy" and slapping me on the back almost every day as a little girl. My grandmother would say, "If you hit that girl one more time I'm going to call the people on you!" I couldn't bring myself to look that word up in the dictionary until I was 40 years old. I had an idea of what it meant, and I thought of looking it up a few times throughout my life, but I wouldn't allow myself to go there. I was afraid of what my mom thought of me, even as a woman of God.

When I finally googled that word, I thought, "Oh that's not what I am now and that's not what I was then. I thought to myself, okay, I'm good. I was able to move beyond the hurt that word caused.

Knowing that I'm not wounded anymore means that I can just be Katina; take my good with my bad. I didn't wound my own soul as a child and it wasn't even about me, it was about the people who wounded me. I take responsibility for my bad decisions stemming from those wounds and I can just breathe in God's goodness knowing I'm forgiven. I accept my past because it prepared me for where I am today.

When we accept what we've been through, we come into a more peaceful existence. Beauty for Ashes becomes a relatable Bible verse. The significance of something being ashes is like lifting a balloon into the air and watching it fly away. Ashes have absolutely no chance of being revived!

Visualize your past hurts and pains, your wounds burning, becoming ashes. Release it to God and watch God replace the ashes with beauty. Watch the Lord's grace restore your soul. You are more than a conqueror, victorious, and amazing in the eyes of the Lord!

I hope this book brought you a message from God. I also hope that you will use that message to bless others. What I would like to end with is this: Everything you went through prepared you for the position you are in right now and what you are going through right now is preparing you for your next position. Don't give up! You are useful to the Body of Christ. You have a story, share it, and surrender your mess for a message. Be Blessed!

The Book of Philippians

My favorite book of the Bible is Philippians. It is a
profound letter written by Paul while he was in prison.
I've read this book several times and God always speaks to
me with a new message for the season of life I'm in. I
hope God speaks to you through this beautiful book so that
you may enjoy it as much I do!

Philippians 1

1 Paul and Timotheus, the servants of Jesus Christ, to all
the saints in Christ Jesus which are at Philippi, with the
bishops and deacons:
2 Grace be unto you, and peace, from God our Father, and
from the Lord Jesus Christ.
3 I thank my God upon every remembrance of you,
4 Always in every prayer of mine for you all making
request with **joy**,
5 For your fellowship in the gospel from the first day until
now;
6 Being confident of this very thing, that he which hath
begun a good work in you will perform it until the day of
Jesus Christ:

This is one of the most popular verses in the Bible because
it projects a spirit of encouragement. It tells us to be
confident in knowing that God will see us through till the
end of time, we can draw strength from this verse when
our spirit is not sure what's next or when we feel like
giving up.

⁷ Even as it is meet for me to think this of you all, because I have you in my heart; in as much as both in my bonds, and in the defense and confirmation of the gospel, ye all are partakers of my grace.

⁸ For God is my record, how greatly I long after you all in the bowels of Jesus Christ.

⁹ And this I pray, that your love may abound yet more and more in knowledge and in all judgment;

¹⁰ That ye may approve things that are excellent; that ye may be sincere and without offence till the day of Christ.

¹¹ Being filled with the fruits of righteousness, which are by Jesus Christ, unto the glory and praise of God.

¹² But I would ye should understand, brethren, that the things which happened unto me have fallen out rather unto the furtherance of the gospel;

¹³ So that my bonds in Christ are manifest in all the palace, and in all other places;

¹⁴ And many of the brethren in the Lord, waxing confident by my bonds, are much more bold to speak the word without fear.

¹⁵ Some indeed preach Christ even of envy and strife; and some also of good will:

¹⁶ The one preach Christ of contention, not sincerely, supposing to add affliction to my bonds:

¹⁷ But the other of love, knowing that I am set for the defense of the gospel.

¹⁸ What then? notwithstanding, every way, whether in pretense, or in truth, Christ is preached; and I therein do rejoice, yea, and will rejoice.

¹⁹ For I know that this shall turn to my salvation through your prayer, and the supply of the Spirit of Jesus Christ,

²⁰ According to my earnest expectation and my hope, that in nothing I shall be ashamed, but that with all boldness, as

always, so now also Christ shall be magnified in my body, whether it be by life, or by death.

[21] For to me to live is Christ, and to die is gain.

[22] But if I live in the flesh, this is the fruit of my labor: yet what I shall choose I wot not.

[23] For I am in a strait betwixt two, having a desire to depart, and to be with Christ; which is far better:[24] Nevertheless to abide in the flesh is more needful for you.

[25] And having this confidence, I know that I shall abide and continue with you all for your furtherance and joy of faith;

[26] That your rejoicing may be more abundant in Jesus Christ for me by my coming to you again.

[27] Only let your conversation be as it becometh the gospel of Christ: that whether I come and see you, or else be absent, I may hear of your affairs, that ye stand fast in one spirit, with one mind striving together for the faith of the gospel;

[28] And in nothing terrified by your adversaries: which is to them an evident token of perdition, but to you of salvation, and that of God.

[29] For unto you it is given in the behalf of Christ, not only to believe on him, but also to suffer for his sake;

[30] Having the same conflict which ye saw in me, and now hear to be in me.

Notes_____

_____

_____

2 If there be therefore any consolation in Christ, if any comfort of love, if any fellowship of the Spirit, if any bowels and mercies,

² Fulfil ye my joy, that ye be likeminded, having the same love, being of one accord, of one mind.

³ Let nothing be done through strife or vainglory; but in lowliness of mind let each esteem other better than themselves.

⁴ Look not every man on his own things, but every man also on the things of others.

⁵ Let this mind be in you, which was also in Christ Jesus:

⁶ Who, being in the form of God, thought it not robbery to be equal with God:

⁷ But made himself of no reputation, and took upon him the form of a servant, and was made in the likeness of men:

⁸ And being found in fashion as a man, he humbled himself, and became obedient unto death, even the death of the cross.

⁹ Wherefore God also hath highly exalted him, and given him a name which is above every name:

¹⁰ That at the name of Jesus every knee should bow, of things in heaven, and things in earth, and things under the earth;

¹¹ And that every tongue should confess that Jesus Christ is Lord, to the glory of God the Father.

¹² Wherefore, my beloved, as ye have always obeyed, not as in my presence only, but now much more in my absence, work out your own salvation with fear and trembling.

¹³ For it is God which worketh in you both to will and to do of his good pleasure.

¹⁴ Do all things without murmurings and disputings:

¹⁵ That ye may be blameless and harmless, the sons of God, without rebuke, in the midst of a crooked and perverse nation, among whom ye shine as lights in the world;

¹⁶ Holding forth the word of life; that I may rejoice in the day of Christ, that I have not run in vain, neither laboured in vain.

¹⁷ Yea, and if I be offered upon the sacrifice and service of your faith, I joy, and rejoice with you all.

¹⁸ For the same cause also do ye joy, and rejoice with me.

¹⁹ But I trust in the Lord Jesus to send Timotheus shortly unto you, that I also may be of good comfort, when I know your state.

²⁰ For I have no man likeminded, who will naturally care for your state.

²¹ For all seek their own, not the things which are Jesus Christ's.

²² But ye know the proof of him, that, as a son with the father, he hath served with me in the gospel.

²³ Him therefore I hope to send presently, so soon as I shall see how it will go with me.

²⁴ But I trust in the Lord that I also myself shall come shortly.

²⁵ Yet I supposed it necessary to send to you Epaphroditus, my brother, and companion in labour, and fellowsoldier, but your messenger, and he that ministered to my wants.

²⁶ For he longed after you all, and was full of heaviness, because that ye had heard that he had been sick.

²⁷ For indeed he was sick nigh unto death: but God had mercy on him; and not on him only, but on me also, lest I should have sorrow upon sorrow.

28 I sent him therefore the more carefully, that, when ye see him again, ye may rejoice, and that I may be the less sorrowful.

29 Receive him therefore in the Lord with all gladness; and hold such in reputation:

30 Because for the work of Christ he was nigh unto death, not regarding his life, to supply your lack of service toward me.

Notes

_____

_____

_____

_____

_____

_____

_____

_____

Philippians 3

3 Finally, my brethren, rejoice in the Lord. To write the same things to you, to me indeed is not grievous, but for you it is safe.

² Beware of dogs, beware of evil workers, beware of the concision.

³ For we are the circumcision, which worship God in the spirit, and rejoice in Christ Jesus, and have no confidence in the flesh.

⁴ Though I might also have confidence in the flesh. If any other man thinketh that he hath whereof he might trust in the flesh, I more:

⁵ Circumcised the eighth day, of the stock of Israel, of the tribe of Benjamin, an Hebrew of the Hebrews; as touching the law, a Pharisee;

⁶ Concerning zeal, persecuting the church; touching the righteousness which is in the law, blameless.

⁷ But what things were gain to me, those I counted loss for Christ.

⁸ Yea doubtless, and I count all things but loss for the excellency of the knowledge of Christ Jesus my Lord: for whom I have suffered the loss of all things, and do count them but dung, that I may win Christ,

⁹ And be found in him, not having mine own righteousness, which is of the law, but that which is through the faith of Christ, the righteousness which is of God by faith:

¹⁰ That I may know him, and the power of his resurrection, and the fellowship of his sufferings, being made conformable unto his death;

¹¹ If by any means I might attain unto the resurrection of the dead.

¹² Not as though I had already attained, either were already perfect: but I follow after, if that I may apprehend that for which also I am apprehended of Christ Jesus.

¹³ Brethren, I count not myself to have apprehended: but this one thing I do, forgetting those things which are behind, and reaching forth unto those things which are before,

¹⁴ I press toward the mark for the prize of the high calling of God in Christ Jesus.

¹⁵ Let us therefore, as many as be perfect, be thus minded: and if in any thing ye be otherwise minded, God shall reveal even this unto you.

¹⁶ Nevertheless, whereto we have already attained, let us walk by the same rule, let us mind the same thing.

¹⁷ Brethren, be followers together of me, and mark them which walk so as ye have us for an ensample.

¹⁸ (For many walk, of whom I have told you often, and now tell you even weeping, that they are the enemies of the cross of Christ:

¹⁹ Whose end is destruction, whose God is their belly, and whose glory is in their shame, who mind earthly things.)

²⁰ For our conversation is in heaven; from whence also we look for the Saviour, the Lord Jesus Christ:

²¹ Who shall change our vile body, that it may be fashioned like unto his glorious body, according to the working whereby he is able even to subdue all things unto himself.

*Notes*_____

_____

_____

4 Therefore, my brethren dearly beloved and longed for, my joy and crown, so stand fast in the Lord, my dearly beloved.

[2] I beseech Euodias, and beseech Syntyche, that they be of the same mind in the Lord.

[3] And I intreat thee also, true yokefellow, help those women which laboured with me in the gospel, with Clement also, and with other my fellowlabourers, whose names are in the book of life.

[4] Rejoice in the Lord always: and again I say, Rejoice.

[5] Let your moderation be known unto all men. The Lord is at hand.

[6] Be careful for nothing; but in every thing by prayer and supplication with thanksgiving let your requests be made known unto God.

[7] And the peace of God, which passeth all understanding, shall keep your hearts and minds through Christ Jesus.

[8] Finally, brethren, whatsoever things are true, whatsoever things are honest, whatsoever things are just, whatsoever things are pure, whatsoever things are lovely, whatsoever things are of good report; if there be any virtue, and if there be any praise, think on these things.

[9] Those things, which ye have both learned, and received, and heard, and seen in me, do: and the God of peace shall be with you.

[10] But I rejoiced in the Lord greatly, that now at the last your care of me hath flourished again; wherein ye were also careful, but ye lacked opportunity.

[11] Not that I speak in respect of want: for I have learned, in whatsoever state I am, therewith to be content.

¹² I know both how to be abased, and I know how to abound: everywhere and in all things I am instructed both to be full and to be hungry, both to abound and to suffer need.

¹³ I can do all things through Christ which strengtheneth me.

¹⁴ Notwithstanding ye have well done, that ye did communicate with my affliction.

¹⁵ Now ye Philippians know also, that in the beginning of the gospel, when I departed from Macedonia, no church communicated with me as concerning giving and receiving, but ye only.

¹⁶ For even in Thessalonica ye sent once and again unto my necessity.

¹⁷ Not because I desire a gift: but I desire fruit that may abound to your account.

¹⁸ But I have all, and abound: I am full, having received of Epaphroditus the things which were sent from you, an odour of a sweet smell, a sacrifice acceptable, wellpleasing to God.

¹⁹ But my God shall supply all your need according to his riches in glory by Christ Jesus.

²⁰ Now unto God and our Father be glory for ever and ever. Amen.

²¹ Salute every saint in Christ Jesus. The brethren which are with me greet you.

²² All the saints salute you, chiefly they that are of Caesar's household.

²³ The grace of our Lord Jesus Christ be with you all. Amen.

Notes

Preparation

_____

_____

_____

Position

_____

_____

_____

Testimony

_____

_____

_____

_____

Preparation

Position

Testimony

Preparation

_____

_____

_____

_____

Position

_____

_____

_____

_____

Testimony

_____

_____

_____

_____

_____

_____

I'm so deeply grateful to God for giving me the courage and words to write this book. That courage was expanded into starting my own company, Living Faith Empowered. It was birthed after writing this book.

The purpose of my company is to bring women together for sisterhood and the Word of God. It is not work, but my passion and service to God. God is moving and being glorified through Living Faith Empowered and I couldn't ask for anything more gratifying.

TO GOD BE THE GLORY!

Katina L. Brown
Founder & CEO
Living Faith Empowered, LLC

Contact me. I'd love to hear your response to my book:

Visit my website: LivingFaithEmpowered.com
Email: livingfaithempowered@gmail.com
Twitter: @klbpositiveener

Bible Verses

The Holy Bible, King James Version. Cambridge Edition: 1769; King James Bible Online, 2017. www.kingjamesbibleonline.org.

www.ingramcontent.com/pod-product-compliance
Lightning Source LLC
Chambersburg PA
CBHW071430040426
42445CB00012BA/1325